DAY OF THE DEAD

SUGAR SKULLS

ANTI-STRESS COLORING BOOK

ILLUSTRATED BY ANTONY BRIGGS

this book belongs to:

□□□□□□□□□□□□□□□□□□□□□□□□□□□□□□

COMPLICATED
COLORING
www.complicatedcoloring.com

PUBLISHED BY COMPLICATED COLORING

COMPLICATED COLORING
www.complicatedcoloring.com

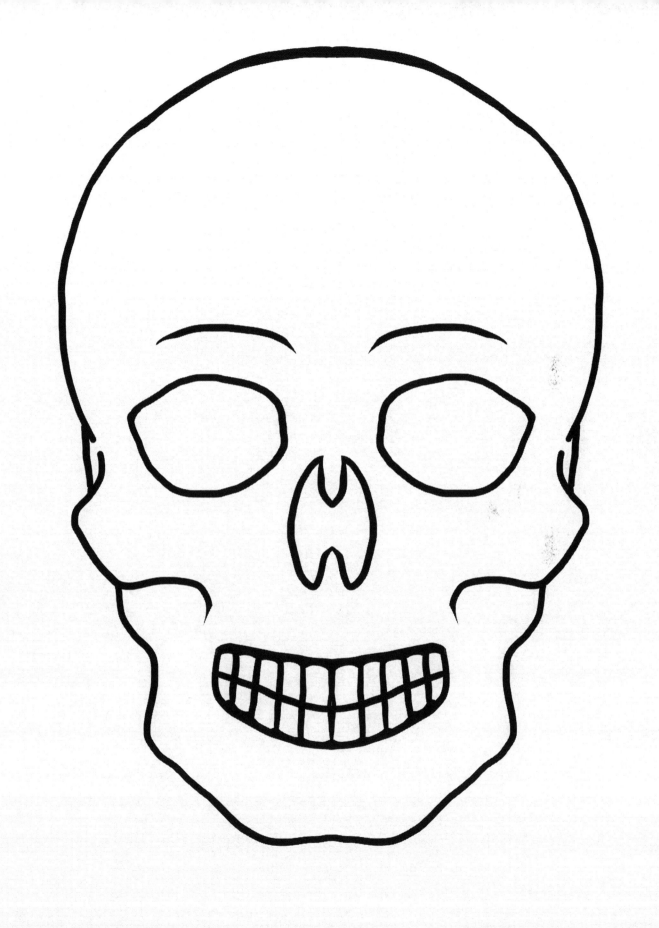

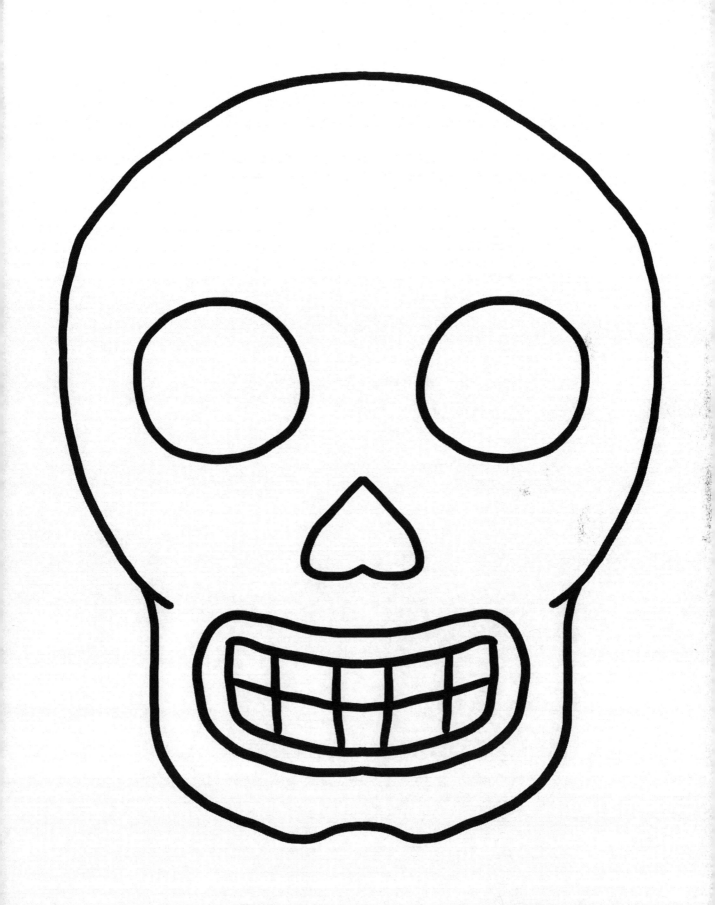

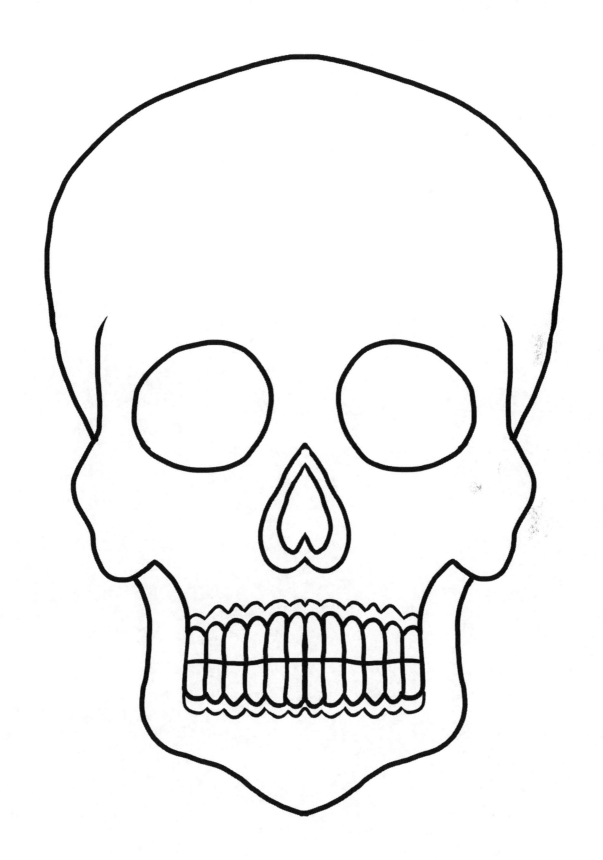

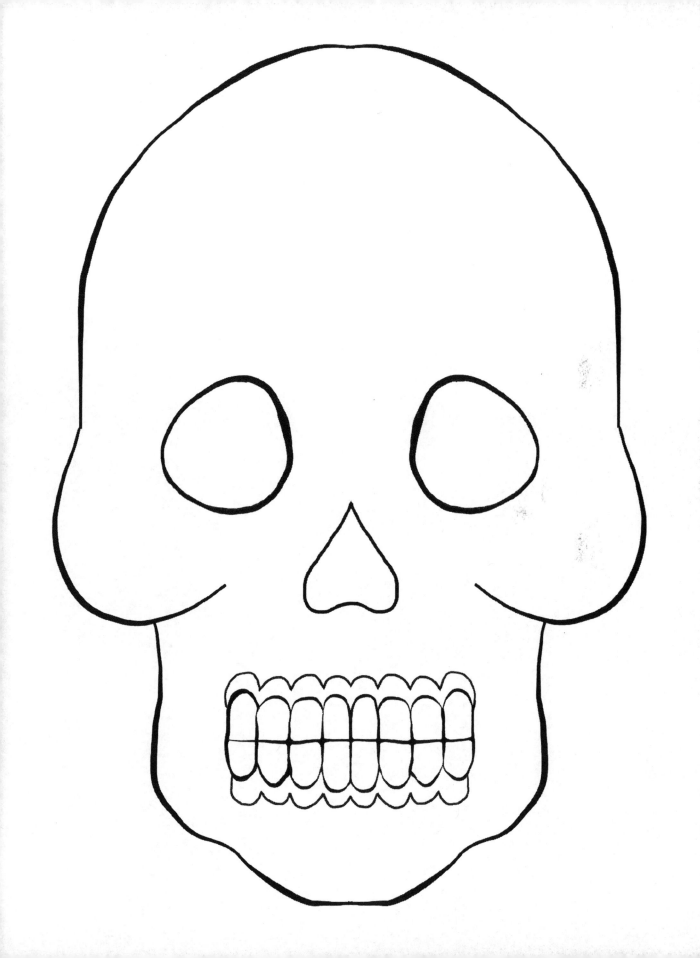

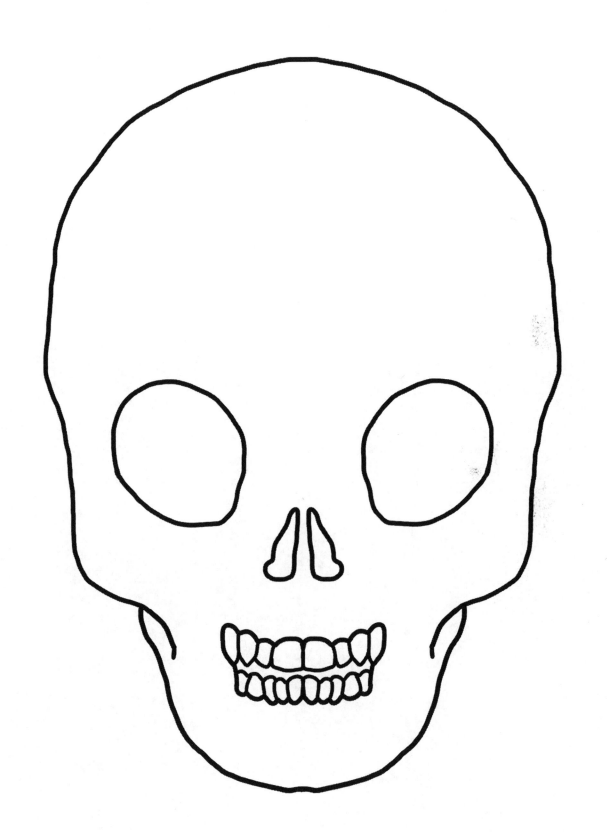

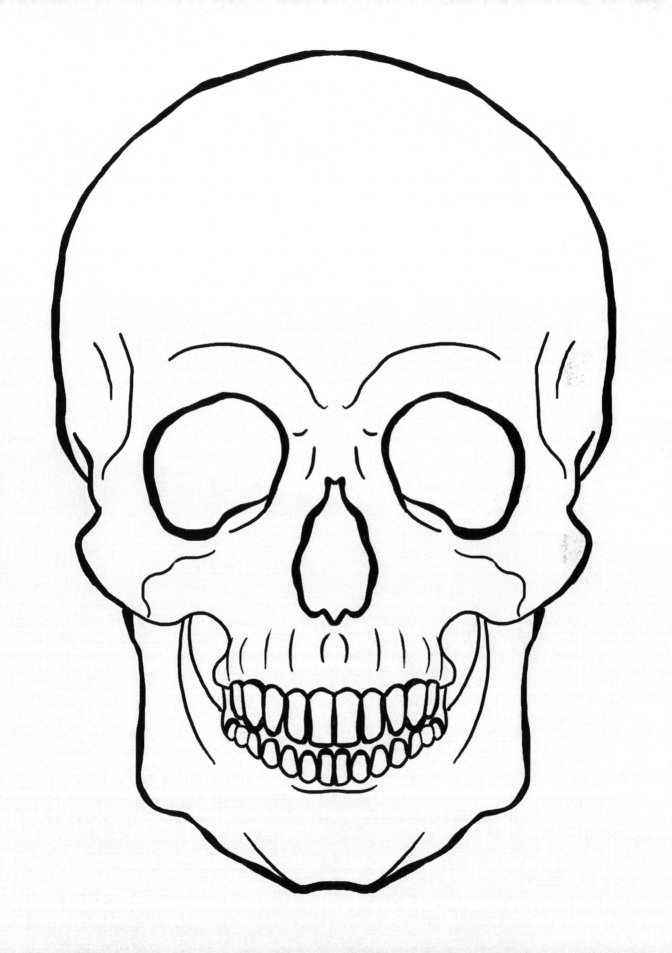

BOOKS IN THIS SERIES:

SHARE ONLINE
WE LOVE TO SEE YOUR COMPLETED MASTERPIECES

 FACEBOOK.COM/COLORING.BOOKS.FOR.GROWN.UPS/

OR

@COMPLICATEDCOLORING

YOU CAN ALSO SHARE PHOTOS OF
YOUR WORK IN AN AMAZON REVIEW.

VISIT OUR WEBSITE:
WWW.COMPLICATEDCOLORING.COM
FOR
UP-TO-DATE NEWS & RELEASES, T-SHIRTS,
POSTERS & FREE PRINTABLE PAGES.

Made in the USA
Lexington, KY
06 March 2016